life MONEY

...in smaller bites

OPTIONS
FOR
NEWBIES

CALL OPTIONS

- Buying Call Options
- Selling Covered Calls
- Spreads
- LEAPS

YAEL EYLAT-TANAKA

DISCLAIMER

This book is written for educational purposes only. No recommendations are made for specific stocks or options strategies. Any stocks, stock symbols, option strategies or illustrations of profit and loss are to be considered as strictly educational examples. Please do your own due diligence; study all available resources, and consult with a broker if necessary. Be aware that trading stocks, options or any combination thereof can be risky – as can anything else in life. Trade at your own risk. Practice paper trading before committing real money to any trade. The results described herein are for illustration purposes only. The deeper your understanding of the concepts, the safer and more certain will be the return *of* your money, as Will Rogers might have said. Please study the concepts thoroughly, and if something is not clear, peruse the index and list of references for more information.

ACKNOWLEDGMENTS

I owe a debt of gratitude to my colleague, John E. Christ, MD, Ph.D. for his assistance in my efforts to distill complicated information into easily understandable language, and present these concepts in logical sequence.

Other Books by this author

*LifeMONEY ... in smaller bites – Options for Newbies –
    CALL OPTIONS – Book 3
LifeMONEY ... in smaller bites – Options for Newbies –
    PUT OPTIONS – Book 4*

*TO THE READER: M. Carling is my alter ego assumed for
the following books of fiction.*

*Time Travel
And Then There Were None
Windswept Dunes: The Burning Heart
Windswept Dunes: The Singing Sands (released 2016)
Windswept Dunes: Chameleon (released 2016)*

*Works identified by (K,p,a) are available in Kindle, print
and audio format.*

Copyright

Published by: Yaël Eylat-Tanaka
Tampa, Florida
Website: Options For Newbies
http://selling-puts.blogspot.com
Email: OptionsforNewbies@outlook.com

Contents

DISCLAIMER
OTHER BOOKS BY THIS AUTHOR
COPYRIGHT
GET THIS BOOK *FREE!*
PREFACE
THE SCOPE OF THIS BOOK

PART I

INTRODUCTION TO OPTIONS
The Basics of All Options
Some Characteristics of All Options
Factors to Consider
Factors That Influence an Option's Price
    In the Money/Out of the Money/At the Money
    Intrinsic Value versus Time Value
    Volatility
    Time Left to Expiration

THE MECHANICS OF A TRADE
Opening a Brokerage Account
Funding Your Account
Trading Levels
Placing a Trade
Order Information
How to Place a Trade

PART II

CALLS AND PUTS
CALL OPTIONS
    Test Your Knowledge
    Why Call Options Are So Popular
    Why Buy Call Options

Limited risk

Unlimited gains

Breakeven

Test Your Knowledge

PART III

STRATEGIES
Strategy: Buying Calls
Strategy: Buying Deep-In-The-Money Calls
    Test Your Knowledge
Strategy: Selling (Covered) Calls
    Test Your Knowledge

EPILOGUE
LEXICON
ACRONYMS AND ABBREVIATIONS
REFERENCES
ABOUT THE AUTHOR
MEMOIRS OF A HUMBLED TRADER

GET THIS BOOK *FREE!*

<u>Click here</u> to receive a **FREE** copy of this book with my compliments, or go directly to <u>http://pro-wordsmith.net</u> and sign up.

PREFACE

I wrote my previous book, *LifeMONEY: Options for Newbies*, with a view to address the vast misconceptions about trading options. As I stated in that book, too many people relegate options trading to the heap of misinformation or downright lies. I do not mean to say that those lies are deliberate; simply that they may be promulgated by folks who have either no understanding of the process, have lost a significant amount of money by trading the wrong strategies, or have heard so-called "experts" spout generalizations. Generalizations are what gave rise to political correctness, an attempt at modifying people's thinking and behaviors so as not to lump an entire group in a certain light, typically unflattering.

The same is true of options. If one has attempted to trade options and lost money, it behooves that person to examine the strategy utilized and the level of attention paid. Options are merely financial instruments – they do not have a life independent of the trader. They are not financial weapons of mass destruction. They are merely instruments, and as with all instruments – be they weapons or cooking utensils, one should know how to manipulate and handle them to best effect. If you attempt to make an omelet on your barbecue grill and the beaten eggs fall through the grate, you cannot blame the grate or the eggs!

Sadly, very little financial education is provided in our schools. Yet financial savvy is critical to all adults in our society. How to budget, how to invest, how to plan for retirement are grave issues that people must address. Leaving those details unexamined or in the hands of others might be the surest path to losing control over one's money and future.

THE SCOPE OF THIS BOOK

This book is a follow-up to Book 2 in the series, LifeMONEY. Book 2, Options for Newbies, described various strategies and concepts directed at the neophyte, all within a single volume.

Although the book itself is short, it may still represent an overwhelming amount of information to soft through. For that reason, I decided to present these strategies and the concepts behind them in bite-sized morsels. The strategies themselves appear as part of the title, and may be easier to pluck as a single read.

I urge you to study these concepts; read as much as you can; study other books that describe these strategies and concepts from different angles; work out some numbers on paper, until you have the mechanics and concepts well entrenched in your mind. Only when you consider yourself competent should you commit real money to any strategy.

One of the most thorough explanations of options can be found at The Options Industry Council (http://optionseducation.org).

Brokerage commissions were not taken into account in the examples given herein.

PART I

INTRODUCTION TO OPTIONS

The purpose of this book is to present technical definitions and distill complicated concepts of options and strategies to their most integral components. There are a number of strategies that make options trading worthwhile, and each of these strategies has several moving parts, including such concepts as Time Value, Intrinsic Value, premium, strike price and the so-called Greeks. Do not let these terms boggle your mind. They are easy to learn and apply, just like the terminology in a game of chess. I break things down to their most elementary components. I encourage you to refer to the Lexicon in the back of this book as often as necessary until they become second nature.

The predominant benefit of options is that they are much less costly than the stocks themselves. Reduced cost can be a treacherous seductress, however, and many a trader has lost a fortune because of the seemingly low cost of entry.

If there is one word that characterizes options, it would be leverage. Leverage is a double-edged sword: Your gains are magnified, but so are your losses.

For example, purchasing 100 shares of XYZ might cost $10,000 for 100 shares, while buying a call option would cost a fraction of that to control the same 100 shares. Needless to say, spending less is much more appealing, and you are still controlling the same 100 shares. This is graphically demonstrated in the following grids:

Buying stock

Price	#shares	Cost
$100	100	$10,000

Buying a call option

Price	#Contracts	Cost
$3	1	$300

The $300 quoted in the above table is arbitrary. Options are priced according to several factors defined and explained below. When considering an options trade, one is guided not only by the price of the option (called the premium), but also by such factors as strike price and how much time is left to expiration. These terms are defined in the Lexicon, as well as in the explanations of the strategies.

Options are contracts, and each options contract controls 100 shares of stock. Options premiums are listed as if for single shares. Therefore, the $3 in the above table represents a single share, but the full cost of one contract would be multiplied by 100 to yield $300.

The Basics of All Options

Let me emphasize a few characteristics of *all* options:

- Options have expiration dates.
- Options are priced in premiums.
- Option premiums are not static.
- Each option contract controls 100 shares
- Option premiums are affected by various factors:
  - ✓ Time to expiration
  - ✓ Volatility
  - ✓ Price of parent stock

Some Characteristics of All Options

Options have characteristics that their parent stocks lack. Some of their characteristics include, but are not limited to, the following:

- Options are a wasting asset. They have a limited lifespan as short as a few days to as long as two years or more. Options typically expire on the third Friday of the month.

- Options have strike prices. When you buy or sell an option, you do so at a specific strike price.

- Options are mostly "American" style, which means they can be exercised anytime from their initiation to their expiration ("European" style options, by contrast, can only be exercised on expiration).

Let's go on a slight tangent before diving into specific options, their definitions and how they function.

Factors to Consider

When you contemplate an options position, there are several factors that should enter your analysis:

- The price of the parent stock
- The expiration date of the option under consideration
- The strike price of the option
- The premium.

Take a look at the table below. It is a screenshot of the options table for Apple Computer (AAPL). The closing price is denoted in the red circle as $95.89. The purple arrow points to Sep16 Calls, signifying that this portion of the table lists call options that expire in September 2016. The green arrow points to the number 2.87 listed in the green "Ask" column. Options premiums omit the dollar sign ($), so "2.87" means $2.87. Horizontally across from that figure, encircled in blue, is the strike price of 97.50. Again, strike prices omit the $. In this example, if you were to BUY the Sep16 97.50 call option, you would pay $2.87 per share, for a total of $287 for a single contract. Options trade in contracts, with each contract controlling 100 shares. The premiums listed reflect the price for a single share. Please refer to *The Basics of All Options* and *Some Characteristics of All Options*, described below.

	AAPL Options		AAPL Mini Options				
AAPL Expiration Months: JulWk2	Jul16	JulWk4	JulWk5	AugWk1	AugWk2	Aug16	S					
Calls							
Last	Chg	Bid	Ask	Vol	OpInt	Action	Strike
	Sep16 Calls				(74 days to expiration)		AAPL @ 95.89
9.45	0	9.35	9.50	00	649	Trade | Detail	87.50
7.50	0	7.35	7.50	00	1,378	Trade | Detail	90.00
5.70	0	5.60	5.65	00	1,858	Trade | Detail	92.50
4.15	0	4.05	4.1	00	6,368	Trade | Detail	95.00
2.91	0	2.83	2.87	00	4,350	Trade | Detail	97.50
1.93	0	1.88	1.91	00	12,278	Trade | Detail	100.00
0.76	0	0.74	0.76	00	17,733	Trade | Detail	105.00

Bid and Ask

It is important to understand that the reason one is able to trade on the open market is because there *IS* a market. What this means is that a market to buy and sell goods exists, and is managed by market makers. These are individuals who are bound to make a market for stocks and options. The difference between the bid and ask prices is how they make their money. All options chains will display a Bid and Ask price. As a seller, you will receive the lesser amount, and as a buyer, you will pay the higher amount. The difference goes to the market maker. If an option is quoted as "3.30 x 3.35" (as shown below), you as the seller will receive $3.30 (per share) and as a buyer you will pay $3.35. Look again at this screenshot, shown earlier:

Apple Inc

Symbol	Last	Change	Bid	Ask	High
AAPL	98.94	-0.09 ▼	98.77	98.87	99.5

AAPL Options | **AAPL Mini Options**

AAPL Expiration Months: JunWk2 | Jun16 | JunWk4 | JulWk1 | JulWk2 | Jul16 | JulWk4 | Aug16 | Sep16 |

Calls

Last	Chg	Bid	Ask	Vol	OpInt	Action	Strike ▼	Last	Chg
	Aug16 Calls				(72 days to expiration)		AAPL @ 98.94		
10.00	-0.17	9.90	10.05	25	3,427	Trade	Detail	90.00		
7.95	-0.13	7.90	8.05	67	3,057	Trade	Detail	92.50		
6.10	-0.28	6.10	6.2	512	9,104	Trade	Detail	95.00		
4.60	-0.25	4.55		286	8,078	Trade	Detail	97.50		
3.29	-0.21	3.30	3.35	1,371	24,643	Trade	Detail	100.00		
1.55	-0.13	1.55	1.58	894	32,811	Trade	Detail	105.00		
0.67	-0.09	0.67	0.70	1,427	42,422	Trade	Detail	110.00		

Bid and ask prices can vary greatly. The greater the volatility of a stock, the wider the spread.

The Lexicon in the back of this book is a good place to learn the lingo of options. Note in the table above that there is a vertical column in orange listing the Bid premiums and a similar vertical column in green listing the Ask premiums for their respective strike prices listed in the column marked Strike. A simple explanation of the difference in premium (Bid 2.83, Ask 2.87) is that the spread between the Bid and the Ask is the amount paid to the market makers. These are the folks (or more likely corporations) that are mandated to make a market for the smooth buying and selling of all options. For that reason, so that market makers are paid for this service, the buyer of an option pays the higher premium, and the seller of an option receives the lower priced premium.

Options premiums are not static. Whatever price you pay to buy or sell an option will change depending on various factors, including time to expiration, the price of the parent stock and overall volatility.

Factors That Influence an Option's Price

Once an options position is initiated, several factors can influence its price (premium). For example, if you buy an option for $3.35, that price will *not* remain static – it will move up or down depending on various factors, affectionately called the Greeks. Those include

- Intrinsic Value versus Time Value
- Volatility
- How much time remains to expiration

Do not fret about these terms. Like any new enterprise, they will become clearer as you gain familiarity with the topic.

Because of these factors, an options trader must remain alert in order to be able to manipulate his portfolio to best effect. Those who are skillful in this art stand to make a great deal of money.

And making money is at the heart of learning to trade options!

In the Money/Out of the Money/At the Money

A call option is said to be In-The-Money if any portion of its premium is below the current stock price. In the case of put options, the reverse is true. Study the chart below to see how this concept applies to calls and puts (courtesy of Investopedia.com). Note that they are inverse:

	Call	Put
In-the Money (ITM)	The strike price is *below* the stock price	The strike price is *above* the stock price
Out-of-the-Money (OTM)	The strike price is *above* the stock price	The strike price is *below* the stock price
At-the-Money (ATM)	The strike price is the *same* as the stock price	The strike price is the *same* as the stock price

Intrinsic Value versus Time Value

The **Intrinsic Value** is that part of the premium that reflects the actual price of the parent stock. For a call option, it is the part of the premium that is *below* the strike price. The reverse is true for a put option: the Intrinsic Value of a put option is when the parent stock's price is *above* the strike price. Time Value is simply the difference between Intrinsic Value and the current premium:

Time Value = Option Prem. + Strike price - stock price

Volatility

The simplest explanation of volatility is the degree to which a stock rises and falls in response to market events. There are stocks such as Pfizer (PFE), Microsoft (MSFT) and Intel (INTC) that do not move much in a day or week, and those are said to be low-volatility stocks. Stocks such as Tesla (TSLA) or Amazon (AMZN), on the other hand, can have massive moves in a day. At the last earnings report, AMZN soared up by $54 in a day.

Time Left to Expiration

Recall that an options premium is made up of both Intrinsic Value and Time Value. Time Value wastes away with each day that passes, and the erosion is much more dramatic the closer one gets to expiration. See the graph below (courtesy of neuwalir.dnyu.com):

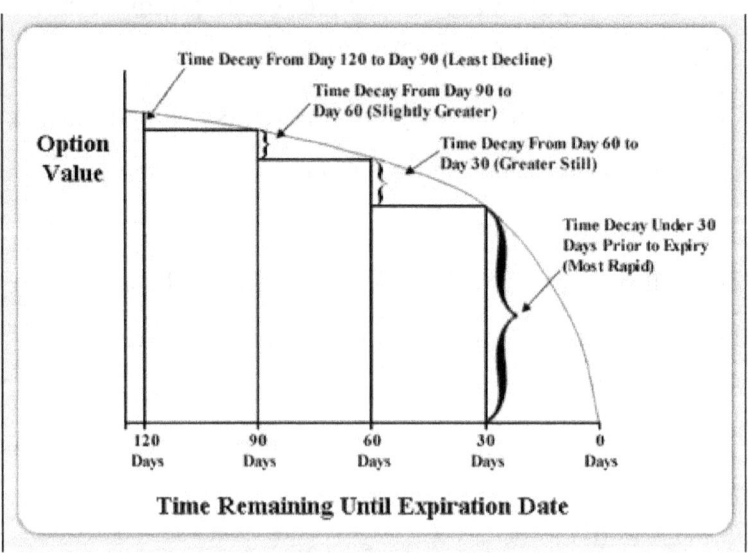

Note that time decay is most rapid in the last 30 days, and gathers speed as it nears expiration.

THE MECHANICS OF A TRADE

When you look at screenshots such as the above, you may wonder how to implement these suggestions. Let me give you a thumbnail sketch.

Opening a Brokerage Account

If you are interested in trading options, you must first open a brokerage account. There are countless options brokers online (see a short list in the Index). I have been using OptionsXpress, and am therefore most familiar with its interface. That will be the source of my examples. I do not specifically recommend this broker – please do your own due diligence and proceed according to your own tastes.

Funding Your Account

You may fund your account with as little as $100. Clearly that will limit your trading ability, since commissions will represent a large percentage of your account. Nevertheless, you ARE able to buy shares of stock or call options. Buying in this case will not be on margin, and will require 100% funding.

Trading Levels

Most brokers – especially those dealing in options trading – assign various levels according to the skill and experience of the new client. The initial level is Level 1 and goes up from there. The higher the level, the greater the options trades permitted. Some strategies, specifically trading naked puts, require a minimum balance to be kept on hand (usually $2,000) as collateral in the event a trade goes against you. Refer to the section on Margin.

Placing a Trade

The stock market – and options market – is open from 9:30 a.m. to 4:00 p.m. Eastern (New York) time. A trade will only be filled during those hours. You may place a trade order at anytime, but it will be executable only during trading hours.

Once you have filled out the necessary forms to open a brokerage account, you will need to fund your account according to the requirements of your chosen broker. When your funds have cleared, you will receive an email advising you that you are ready to trade.

Order Information

Before proceeding, keep in mind the following regarding any option order. You will need to know:

1. Whether you are buying or selling the option;
2. The type of option being bought or sold (call or put);
3. Whether the trade is to open or close the position;
4. The strike price;
5. The expiration date.

How to Place a Trade

Log into your account platform.

From the list of tabs, click on Trade, second from left.

That will bring up the trading window.

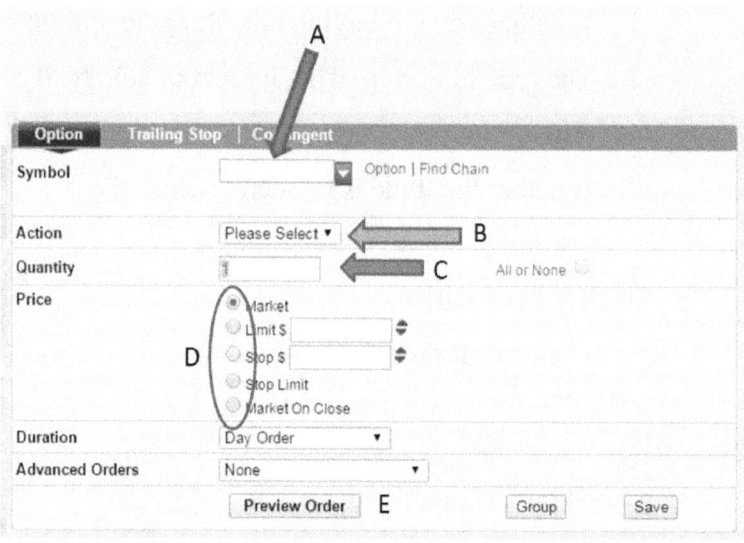

A **Symbol:** Enter the stock symbol. If you don't know it, type the name of the company, and the appropriate symbols will pop up. To the right of the symbol slot are the words Option/Find Chain. Click on Option to get additional information on strike prices and expiration dates.

B **Action:** What kind of a transaction are you entering is reflected in this slot ("Please Select") is a dropdown arrow displaying four options (pardon the pun):

·   Buy to open

·   Buy to close

·   Sell to open

·   Sell to close

Select your desired action (these options will be made clearer as we go on).

C Quantity: Enter how many contracts you wish. The default above is 1. Ignore "All or None."

D Price: For price, the default highlighted is Market. NEVER accept a market price, and instead enter a figure under Limit. Where do you get the figure? From the options chains described above.

E Finally, click **Preview Order**, and the following window will appear:

» Please Review Your Order Carefully

Symbol	Description	Last	Change	Bid	Ask	Volume
AAPL	APPLE INC	99.64	0.70 ▲	99.63	99.64	19,338,170
AAPL Aug16 100 Call	APPLE INC	3.65	0.36 ▲	3.65	3.70	1,450

Action	Qty	Symbol	Description	Contract Size	Price	Duration	All or None
Buy To Open	1	AAPL Aug16 100 Call	APPLE INC	100	Limit 3.35	Day Order	Off

Estimated Commission	$7.60
Estimated Order Total	$342.60
Time	2:18:24 PM ET

This Preview is provided for your protection, so please review all order details carefully. Clicking the "Place Order >>" button will transmit this order to the exchange marketplace for action.

[Cancel] [<< Change]   [Place Order >>]

Be sure to review the information, then click "Place Order"

The mechanics of placing any trade are essentially the same for any type of trade you make, whether you buy or sell stock or option or create spreads (more on spreads under the strategy section). The order windows may look slightly different, but the general premise will be the same. You will see illustrations of trade windows throughout this book.

Once you have placed some trades in your account, your Account Overview will appear, as in the example below:

⊟ Account Balances

Account Value

Current Position Value

Money Markets & Cash[1]

Stock Buying Power

Option Buying Power

⊟ Account Positions

Symbol	Description	Qty	Price
LLY	ELI LILLY AND CO	102.61	$73.86
LLY Jul16 72.5 Put	Eli Lilly and Co	1	$1.53
LLY Jul16 75 Put	Eli Lilly and Co	-1	$2.65

Your positions will appear in the section Account Positions. You may adjust the columns and information displayed to suit your tastes. The above table indicates that the trader owns 102.61 shares of LLY, is "long" (owns) 1 contract of the Jul16 72.5 Put and is "short" (sold) -1 contract of the Jul16 75 Put. These are listed under Qty. If you are "long" an option or stock, the Qty will be a positive number (1); if you are "short" an option or stock, Qty will show a negative number (-1). To reiterate,

LLY Jul16 72.5 Put   1
LLY Jul16 75 Put   -1

Just as in chess, the trick is not in the mechanics, but rather in the art of selecting the proper type of option (call or put) and in your outlook in order to implement the proper strategy.

PART II

CALLS AND PUTS

Options come in two flavors: Calls and Puts.

Both Calls and Puts can be bought and sold. You therefore have a quadrangle of sorts. However, there are many more possibilities and potential combinations from these four positions. This book will elucidate the basic steps.

Calls and Puts are names given to option contracts. The definition of an option is rather straightforward:

An option is the right - but not the obligation - to buy or sell stock at a certain price by a certain date.

Take a look at the following table that describes the definition in more detail.

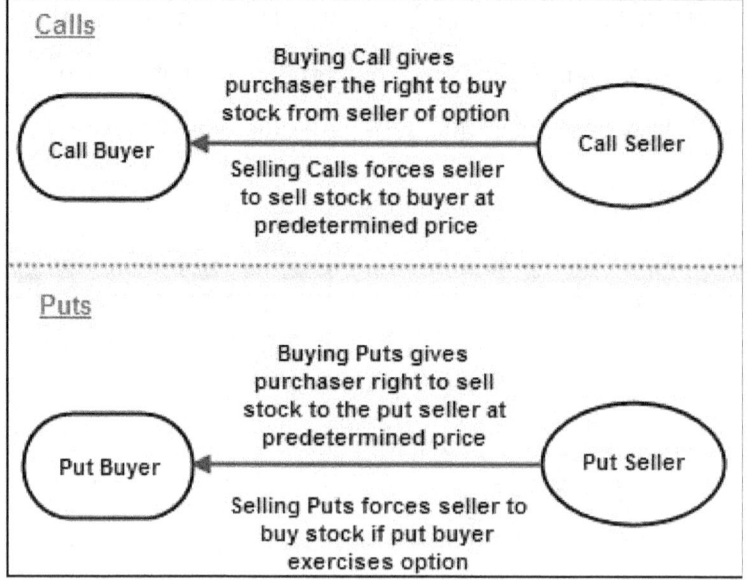

There is another important grid that would be useful here:

CALLS follow the stock price. If the stock goes up, calls go up; if the stock goes down, calls go down.

PUTS are inverse to the stock price. If the stock goes up, puts go down; if the stock goes down, puts go up.

See the chart below:

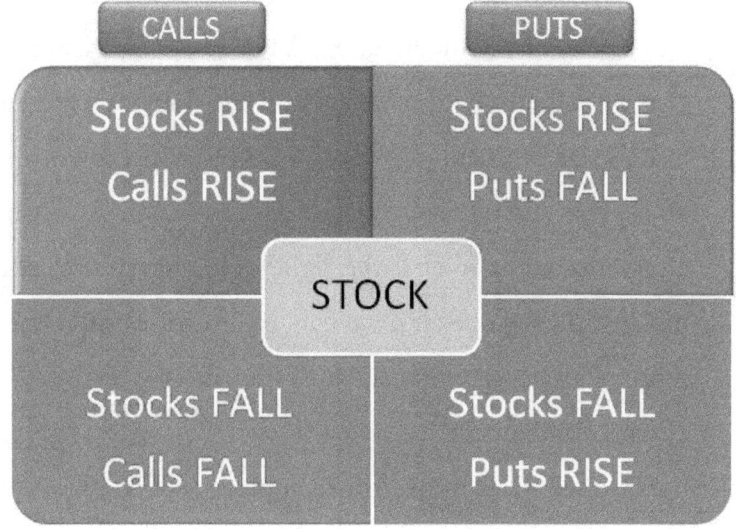

Here is another graphic that may help you remember.

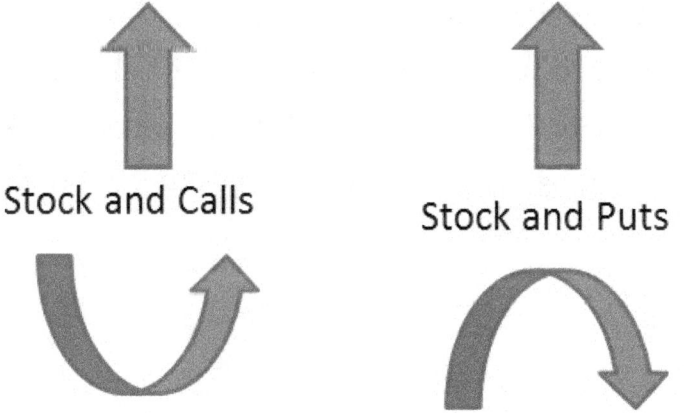

Calls go in the direction of the parent stock's price, while puts are inverse.

If you buy something, say a toaster, you pay money for it and are therefore its owner. You can do with it whatever you please. The seller of the toaster receives money and has an obligation to deliver the toaster. In the world of options, a buyer of an option has the right to do with it as he/she pleases; he/she does not have an obligation to do anything with the option, but the seller of the option does have a certain obligation – to deliver the goods.

Let's look at a specific example.

Call Options

A call option is the right to buy. As previously stated, you may be an owner of that right or the seller of that right.

Call options move in the direction of the parent stock, and their premiums are comprised of **Time Value**, as well as **Intrinsic Value**, the "meat" of the parent stock. Look at the following graph (courtesy of nestedinterest.com):

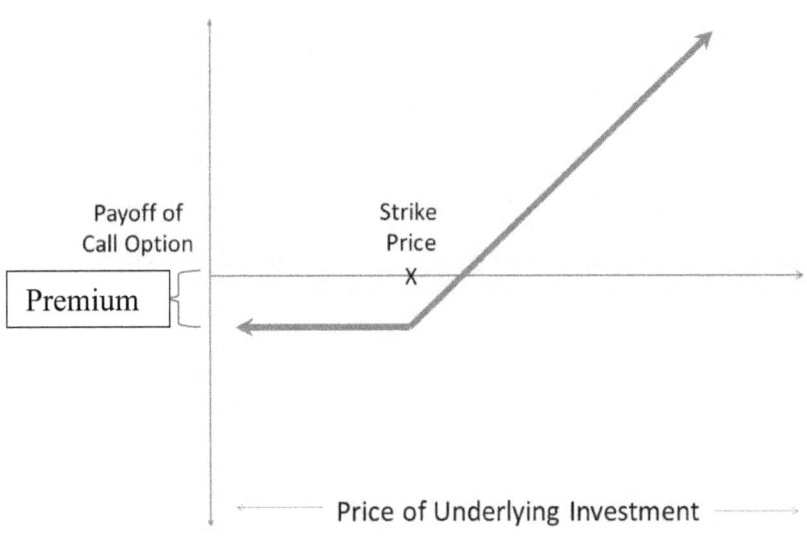

Payoff of
Call Option

Strike
Price

X

Premium

Price of Underlying Investment

The above graph depicts the trajectory of a call option (blue line) rising as the stock price rises (bottom line). Note that if the price of the parent declines, the most you can lose is the amount of the premium you paid. If you bought an AAPL call option at a strike of 100 expiring Aug16, the expectation is that the parent stock will make a move upward. Moreover, the parent stock must make its move *within* the life of the option, and the move must be large enough to encompass at least the cost of the option you bought. In the case of our example, AAPL must rise at least to $103 just to break even and get your money back. Options premiums are made up of Intrinsic Value and Time Value. This will be crucial as you move through this study.

For the moment, let's see how Time Value and Intrinsic Value stack up in a grid.

If a stock is currently trading at $100 and you buy a call option with a strike of $95, that option will have $5 of Intrinsic Value. Please study the following grid to get a better understanding of what comprises **Intrinsic** versus **Time Value**.

Stock Price	Strike	Prem.	TimeV	IntrinsicV	Diff
$90	$95	$ 2.25	$2.25	$ 0	- 5
$87	$85	$ 5.40	$3.40	$ 2	+ 2
$93	$85	$ 9.70	$1.70	$ 8	+ 8
$93	$30	$72.00	$9.00	$63	+63

You may design a similar table to test your knowledge and understanding by filling in random numbers for Stock Price, Strike and Prem., then solving for Time V and Intrinsic V.

Notice in the above table that if the stock trades at $90 and you buy a $95 call option, there is 0 Intrinsic Value to the premium; you have bought a call option for $2.25 ($225 because each option controls 100 shares), and the entire amount of $225 is made up of Time Value. The parent stock must rise to $97.25 for you just to break even, and it must do so within the life of the option. That is generally a very high hurdle, and your call option is likely to expire worthless. If it expires, you will have lost your $225.

Notice the stock priced at $87 above. You are buying a call option with a strike of $85. That is known as being In-The-Money (see Lexicon) and in this case, the premium of $5.40 consists of $3.40 of Time Value and $2 of "meat" or Intrinsic Value ($87-$85=$2).

The Intrinsic Value of an option premium can be calculated by how much of the strike price is within the current stock price. If the stock is currently trading at $25 and your strike price is $20, you are $5 within the stock price, and you are said to be In The Money.

This discussion is for Call Options. Put Options are discussed below.

Let us get back to our AAPL example.

AAPL price $98.94
Call option strike: $100

Expiry	Current Price	Prem.	Time Value
Aug16	$98.94	$3.35	$3.35

What does the above table show? It shows that the entire premium of $3.35 (or $335 for 1 contract) is all comprised of Time Value. As time erodes and gets closer to expiration, more of that premium will erode, unless the parent stock makes the expected move up. The breakeven in this case is $103.35

AAPL must move high enough, and with sufficient time left before expiration so that the option you bought would have "meat" left in it (Intrinsic Value) at expiration. If AAPL rises to $110 by expiration, your $100 call option has NO Time Value left in it, and is comprised entirely of Intrinsic Value.

AAPL price rises to $110
Call option strike you bought: $100

Expiry	Current Price	Prem.	Time Value	Intrinsic Value
Aug16	$110	$3.35	$0	$10

Did you see what happened? In the first table, with the stock priced at $98.94 and the call option strike at 100, the entire premium is composed of Time Value. If the stock price remains constant into expiration, the entire option premium that is made up of Time Value exclusively will evaporate and expire worthless. In order to make a profit – or in the brilliant words of Will Rogers, just get your $335 back - the stock must move in the direction you predicted and during the life of the option! It will do you no good at all if AAPL shoots to the moon a day after the option expires! In the example above, if AAPL rises to $110 by expiration, your profit would be $6.65.

Buy to open 1 AAPL call Aug16	$ 3.35
Sell to close 1 AAPL call Aug16	$10.00
Profit	$ 6.65

That is $665 (less commission) on a single contract. The caveat to bear in mind is that options' Time Value erodes, sometimes dramatically, and the odds of the parent stock making such dramatic moves are low. If you must buy call options, I strongly suggest that you buy Deep-In-The-Money call options with enough time to expiration that the parent stock can make a strong move in the direction you predicted. Refer to Chapter III, Strategies.

This might be as good a place as any to present this caveat: DO NOT BUY TIME VALUE; LEARN TO SELL IT INSTEAD.

Why? Because of the preponderance of options that expire because of time erosion. If you sell "time," and that time erodes, you are more likely to be left with the grub stake in your account.

To recap, options are financial instruments that can be used to very good effect in enhancing portfolio returns and also to protect a portfolio. Remember that:

- Options are a wasting asset.
- Options trade in premiums.
- Each option controls 100 shares of the parent stock.
- Options come in two flavors: Calls and Puts.
- 85% of options expire worthless.
- If you must buy call options, buy deep <u>in the money</u> call options.

Because of this characteristic – the time factor in an option premium - it is said that eighty-five percent of all options expire worthless.

If this statistic is true – that eighty-five percent of options expire worthless – would it not make sense to sell options instead? If you sell an option and receive that premium as a credit into your account, and that option expires worthless, does it not follow that the entire premium remains in your account? The takeaway here is that you should learn to SELL options. We will look at how we go about selling options to good effect, with such maneuvers as covered calls, naked puts and credit spreads.

<u>Test Your Knowledge</u>

As a brain teaser, please complete the following grid by placing a check under the appropriate column. These are all call options.

Price	Strike	ITM	OTM	ATM
$95	85			
$75	75			
$32	75			
$56	65			

Why Call Options Are So Popular

The appeal of options is their low cost as compared with the parent stock. In our example, the call option that controls 100 shares of AAPL costs a mere fraction of what would otherwise cost $9,894. If call options represent the right to buy a stock, it follows that you expect the stock to make a move to the upside – otherwise why would you buy it?

Recall from our previous discussion that several factors affect the price of an option.

In our example here, where we bought 1 AAPL call option at a strike of 100 expiring Aug16, we bought a contract giving us the right to buy AAPL at 100 anytime between now and the 3rd Friday in August 2016. As shown above, AAPL closed at $98.94.

If you believe that a stock is headed higher, you may wish to capitalize on that growth by buying a call option. But if you believe a stock is headed higher, why not simply buy the stock itself? The answer is leverage. Options cost a fraction of their parent stock. Apple Computer (AAPL) for example, trades at approximately $100 on the open market. To buy a single share of stock would cost you $100; however, buying a single call option would control 100 shares of AAPL, and depending on the strike price and expiration, might cost you only a fraction of the parent stock, and you would be controlling 100 shares of stock.

What does that mean in practice? If AAPL trades at $98.94 and you believe it is headed higher, you may purchase a call option at a strike of $100 that expires next month. You may pay $3.35 (or $335 for each option contract that controls 100 shares) for the right to buy AAPL anytime between now and expiration next month at your selected strike of $100. If AAPL soars to $110, you have the right to buy the stock at $100, because that was the contract you bought. It does not matter how high AAPL rises – your contract was for $100. One contract, 100 shares, for which you paid $335, would permit you to buy 100 shares of AAPL for $100 ($10,000), and resell it at the market for $110 ($11,000), for a tidy profit of $1000 less the $335 you paid for that right.

Let's break down the above:

- AAPL price $98.94

- Expectation: higher
- Action: Buy a call
  - ✓ Expiry: Next month*
  - ✓ Strike: $100
  - ✓ Premium paid: $3.35
  - ✓ Amount paid: $335 (1 call x100 shares x$3.35)
- Outcome: AAPL rises to $110. You OWN the right to buy it at $100. You buy 100 shares at $10,000, and resell them at $11,000.
- Profit: $1000 - $335 premium paid = $665 profit.
- ROI (return on investment): $335/$665=199%.

*"Next month" is not an expiration date. Options expire on the third Friday of every month. For illustration purposes for this example, we spoke about next month's expiration without selecting a specific month. We will get into specific dates later on.

In this case, you bought the call option, and you therefore own the right to buy the underlying stock (AAPL) for $100 on the open market, regardless how high it goes. This is critical. If AAPL flies to $875, your contract is to buy it for $100 for as long as you own that call option. Remember the definition of an option: the right, but not the OBLIGATION to buy that stock. Of course, with this scenario where AAPL soars to $875, you might very well choose to exercise your right. But you may also wish to simply sell your call option and pocket the profit.

What? Yes. Recall that call options move in the direction of the stock, so if the stock rises in price, theoretically, so does the call option. I say theoretically because the stock must rise sufficiently above the Time Value portion of the option to become profitable.

Look again at the grid for CALLS and PUTS. Let us say you buy a CALL option. If you bought that CALL, you are its owner. As its owner, you have the right – but not the obligation – to BUY its parent stock (100 shares thereof) at any time between now and the option's expiration.

With the numbers described above, you may wonder why I put in that disclaimer – that you do not have an obligation to buy the stock. Are you screaming at me from the other side of your computer, "WHY ON EARTH NOT?!"

Remember that you may buy and sell the options themselves. In the above example, you bought the call option for $3.35 when AAPL was trading at $98.94 on the open market. If you exercise your call and buy AAPL for $100, you would pay $10,000, plus the $335 you paid for the premium. If you wish to own AAPL shares, by all means, exercise your option and buy AAPL at $100. However, some of the characteristics of all options is that their premiums are NOT static. What do you think happens to the call option itself if the parent stock soars in price? That's right: The call option premium rises too, sometimes dramatically.

Since you do not have an *obligation* to buy the parent stock, you might simply sell the call option itself at a fat profit – provided that it, too, has risen in price.

Wait – didn't I just say that options premiums are not static, and if the stock soars, so will the option?

Yes, I did, and this is where things get interesting.

Why Buy Call Options

By now, you are no doubt wondering why not buy AAPL outright, even just a few shares, since the stock itself never expires.

While it is true that the stock does not expire, the company itself can go out of business (ever heard of Enron? RCA? Wrigley's?), as well as suffer significant declines in price, even without becoming obsolete. Remember such venerable names as Intel that reached its height during the Dot Com bubble in the $130's, only to be languishing around $30 for the past fifteen years or so? There have been many such companies with stellar balance sheets and products that have plummeted in price and have yet to recover. If you own shares in any of those companies, you would now be sitting on substantial losses.

That is not to say that owning stock is a bad idea. Not at all. It is simply a discussion of why some people gravitate to options for their many advantages, not the least of which is their lower cost.

Limited risk

If you bought a call option expecting to participate in AAPL rally, but that rally did not materialize, the entire sum you paid for that option is lost. In our example herein, the cost of one contract was $335, and therefore, your option would expire worthless, and you would have lost your grub stake of $335. If you owned 100 shares of AAPL, you would still own the shares at whatever price they closed.

To reiterate, in our example, we bought the Aug16 100 call option when AAPL was trading at $98.94 on the open market. If AAPL meanders between $100 and $98, $96, $101, then back down to $99 by Aug16, your entire premium cost of $335 will be lost. AAPL *must* move at least to $103.35 for you to just break even.

Unlimited gains

Above I described what happens in the event AAPL price declines or remains the same through the Aug16 expiration. But what happens if AAPL stages a furious rally based on some great news? Suppose it flies up to $875 any time before Aug16 expiration? As the owner of the $100 strike call option, you participate in those gains. Remember that an option gives you, its owner, the right to exercise it. No matter how high the parent stock goes, your contract remains at $100 (or whatever strike you choose). You participate dollar for dollar with any gains in the parent stock above your breakeven, $103.35 in this case.

It is this kind of fantastic gain that lures many an unsuspecting fly to the honey.

Breakeven

Breakeven is the amount of premium paid plus the closing price of the parent stock. If the strike price you are buying is 50 and you pay a premium of $1.75, your breakeven will be $51.75, just to get your $1.75 back. To make a profit, the stock must rise above $51.75.

Test Your Knowledge

Figure out your break-even:

Price	Strike	Prem.	B/E
$100	100	3.35	$103.35
$ 96	100	2.4	
$ 72	100	5.7	
$105	100	8.3	

This is the primary reason why people globalize options as risky instruments, failing to understand some basic premises germane to options. Call options require that the parent stock move sufficiently in an upward direction and do so in a timely manner. Buying call options is therefore putting the odds squarely against you. What makes the hurdle even more difficult to overcome is that many traders buy Out-of-The-Money call options. These options create a condition that is almost impossible to overcome because of what is known as the delta, one of the "Greeks," discussed below in Part IV, Other Considerations. Suffice to state that Out-of-The-Money options are made up of Time Value exclusively, and deteriorate rapidly, especially if the parent stock has little volatility. The time erosion becomes much more rapid the closer you get to expiration.

The fantasy of "small losses" is what compels so many traders to be attracted to buying calls. Sadly, many traders have gone broke losing small amounts repeatedly.

Verdict: Don't buy call options, unless they are deep-In-The-Money or part of a spread. See Part III, Strategies.

PART III

STRATEGIES

Strategy: Buying Calls
OUTLOOK: Bullish.

Call options are the right to buy a stock at a predetermined price (strike) by a predetermined date (expiration date). If you anticipate a stock to go higher, you would buy a call option to participate in that upward move.

A call option INCREASES in value as the parent stock's price INCREASES in value.

A bit earlier, in the illustrations pertaining to AAPL, the mock order displayed was to <u>buy to open</u> a call option expiring in Aug16 at a strike price of 100. (By the way, this might be a good place to mention that option chains and stock prices omit the dollar sign; henceforth, I shall follow suit).

As the buyer of that call option, you are its owner, and may do with it as you wish. Specifically, you may:

- Hold onto it with the expectation that it will increase in value;
- Exercise it;
- Roll it out to a future time;
- Roll it out to a different strike price;

- Turn it into a spread.
- Sell it to close.

In any event, you have no obligation to do any of the above.

Above I described some of the factors that influence options pricing, including expiration date, strike price and the price of the parent stock. Another factor is how much time remains until expiration.

Strategy: Buying Deep-In-The-Money Calls
OUTLOOK: Stock substitution

Call options serve as stock substitution. Instead of buying stock outright where the out-of-pocket amount is high, you would buy a call option that tracks the stock movement and lets its owner profit if the stock moves up. For call options to make sense, you would want to buy as much "meat" as possible, e.g., Intrinsic Value. The deeper In-The-Money the call option, the greater the Intrinsic Value. When you buy call options, you want to spend as little as possible on the Time Value portion of the premium.

As an example, consider XYZ stock currently trading at $100 on the open market. If you buy a 100 strike, you are spending money exclusively for Time Value, as no portion of the strike is In-The-Money. However, if you buy a call option with a strike of 90, you are buying $10 worth of Intrinsic Value.

With call options, In-The-Money options have strike prices BELOW the current market price of the parent stock.

Test Your Knowledge

How much Time Value is in the premium?

Current Price	Strike	Premium Pd.	Time Value
$105.32	100	3.55	
$232.00	205	10.66	
$ 78.43	90	5.78	
$ 43.00	55	1.32	

Earlier I urged you to not buy Time Value. What about *selling* Time Value instead?

Strategy: Selling (Covered) Calls
OUTLOOK: Bearish, Neutral and Bullish

Recall my description above, albeit extremely simplistically, that if you buy something, you pay for it, but if you sell something, you receive money.

The strategy of selling calls can easily be described as FREE MONEY. It is a technique for pulling money out of the market on stock you own, which serves to reduce your initial cost.

This strategy is more accurately known as selling covered calls, or covered call writing, and requires that you own at least 100 shares of an optionable stock. Not all stocks have options, and since we are discussing selling a call option, obviously this requires that the parent stock be optionable.

Recall the definition of a call option: It is the right – but not the obligation – to *buy* stock at a predetermined price (the strike price) by a predetermined date (the expiration date).

Let's stay with our example of AAPL, trading at approximately $100. Suppose you have owned your shares for a while, you bought them at $50, or received them as a gift and now for whatever reason you wish to sell your shares to bring in some cash. You could sell AAPL directly to the market (through your brokerage account) and pocket the proceeds. If you are willing to sell those shares, why not sell someone the right to buy them from you?

If you sell a call option, you are obligating yourself to deliver the goods – in this case, your AAPL shares. Instead of delivering AAPL shares to the marketplace directly, you sell someone the right (a contract) to buy those shares from you at a specific price (that you select). For that right, you will be paid a premium.

Why would you do that? To generate a source of income to defray your cost of owning AAPL shares. If AAPL is currently trading at $100, you decide at what price you are willing to sell your shares. Let's stay with our example of the 100 strike. You would *sell* a call option expiring Aug16 with a premium of $3 (of $300 for 100 shares). Please refer back to the options chain above, where will note that the bid/ask premiums are listed as 3.30 x 3.35. To create this trade, you would Sell to Open 1 contract of AAPL expiring Aug16 at a Limit Price of 3.30. Since options contracts control 100 shares, the minimum you can sell is a single contract. The premium of $330 (less commission) is deposited into your account by the next day.

By selling someone the right to buy AAPL at $100 anytime between now and Aug16, you have an obligation to deliver your shares at the strike price no matter how high AAPL goes. That is the downside of covered calls: They limit your upside. On the other hand, they also provide a source of income to mitigate your cost of buying the shares in the first place.

What happens if AAPL rises to $130 by expiration? Your shares will be called away at $100. Your account will reflect a cash infusion of $10,000 (less commission) three days later. You keep the premium. What happens of AAPL declines to $95? Your shares will stay in your account, and you still keep the $330. You may now repeat the process by selling more covered calls at future expirations, at whatever strike you wish.

Following is the risk graph for covered call selling (courtesy of Investopedia):

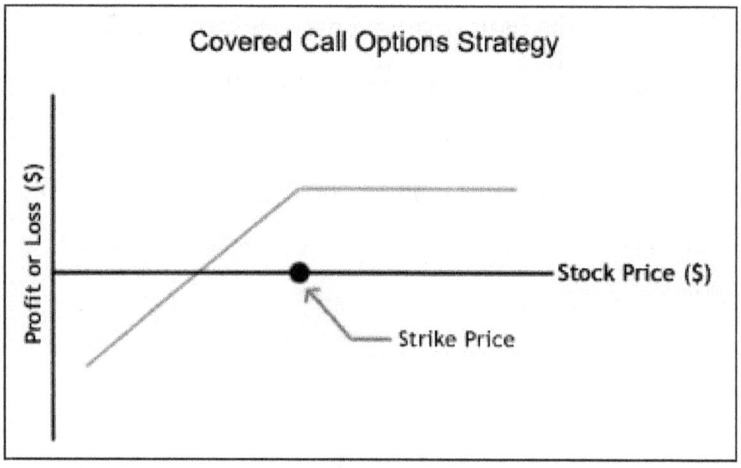

In either case – whether you keep your shares or have them called away – the premium of $330 is yours to keep.

Test Your Knowledge

Price	Strike	Prem.	Price	BE
$93.27	95	3.00	$95.03	
$74.03	70	6.35	$74.00	
$23.00	25	4.15	$33.15	

$54.54	60	8.70	$63.33	

Ini.Price = Price you paid for parent stock.
Cc Prem = Covered call premium
Exp.Price = Price of parent stock at expiration.

Strategy: Bull Call Spreads (Debit)
OUTLOOK: Bullish

One hundred shares of AAPL at $100 per share require a cash outlay of $10,000. From our examples above, the $100 strike price expiring in three months is listed at 3.30 x 3.35, and allows the buyer to control the same 100 shares. If you are bullish on AAPL, and want to participate in an increase in its price, instead of buying 100 shares, you might choose to buy a call option. You might consider buying one contract of the Aug16 100 strike at the listed price of 3.35 (remember, you buy at the ask) and pay $335 (plus commission). To defray that cost, you could sell the equivalent of a covered call on your call option. Just as AAPL is currently trading at $100, so is your call option at the strike of 100. You are the owner of that call, and therefore can sell a "covering" call against it, say the Aug16 105 strike call. Since the 105 strike is Out-of-The-Money (Time Value only), its premium is likely to be much lower, around 1.65 ($165 less commission). Remember, you will receive the bid amount.

		Bid	Ask				
8.00	0	8.05	8.20	00	3,031	Trade | Detail |	92.50
6.30	0	6.25	6.35	00	8,744	Trade | Detail	95.00
4.84	0	4.7	4.80	00	8,137	Trade | Detail	97.50
3.45	0	3	3.50	00	24,493	Trade | Detail	100.00
1.68	0	1.65	1.68	00	34,998	Trade | Detail	105.00
0.75	0	0.74	0.77	00	43,161	Trade | Detail	110.00

What is the effect of this spread?

Buy to open AAPL 1 contract Aug16 100 call   - $335
Sell to open AAPL 1 contract Aug16 105 call   +$165
Total Debit   - $170
(Commissions are omitted).
Margin required: 100% of debit.

The Bull Call Spread is a debit spread because you must pay to create it. The above spread would cost $170 for a single contract. You would open this type of a trade if you are bullish on AAPL between now and the August 2016 expiration. If AAPL price rises above $105, you stand to make the different between the strikes ($105-$100) or $5 ($500 less commission) less the $170 you spent, for a total of $330. Of course, if you trade more than 1 contract, these numbers can multiply dramatically.

The appeal of this strategy is the cost of entry versus the potential gain.

This strategy is called Bull Call Spread because the outlook is bullish; the expectation is for a rise in the price of the parent stock.

Strategy: Bear Call Spreads (Credit)
OUTLOOK: Bearish

The opposite strategy is named appropriately the Bear Call Spread. If you anticipate a decline in prices, you may wish to open a trade that takes advantage of that. For example, suppose AAPL soars overnight by a figure that you do not feel is sustainable, say, to $150. You might open a Bear Call Spread in anticipation of the price retracing to a lower point. Here is what it would look like:

Buy to open AAPL 1 contract Aug16 160 call	- $100
Sell to open AAPL 1 contract Aug16 155 call	+$165
Total Credit	$ 65

Margin required: The difference between spread and premium received.

Bear Call Spreads are credit spreads. You will bring money into your account for taking the risk that AAPL will decline a bit from its "unreasonably" lofty heights. If that does not materialize and AAPL continues upward, the maximum you can lose is the difference between the strikes ($5) or $500 less the credit you received of $65, or $435. Your outlook should be well entrenched before opening this trade. If you go sufficiently Out-of-The-Money and create a call spread that is all Time Value, you stand a good chance of having the spread expire in your favor. In any case, the $65 is deposited in your account the next day. If you open more than a single contract, your credit is multiplied by that number.

Strategy: Adjusting the Legs
OUTLOOK: Correcting or Enhancing a Trade

Recall that a spread involves buying a lower strike and selling a higher strike, or vice versa. Recall, too, that options premiums do not remain static over time, either because of the parent stock's price movement and/or the passage of time. That is true of the buy and sell portions of spreads as well. Take a look at the following table:

Symbol/Description	Quantity	Avg Price	Total Cost	Current Price	Gain/Loss
AAPL Jul16 100 Put	5	8.1	$4,050.00	3.65	-$2,225.00
AAPL Jul16 105 Put	-5	13.22	($6,610.00)	7.5	$2,860.00
TSLA Jun16 225 Put	5	1.54	$771.00	5.25	$1,854.00
TSLA Jun16 227.5 Put	-5	1.97	($985.00)	6.51	-$2,270.00

The spread of AAPL Jul16 100 Put and 105 Put currently displays a $2,860 *profit* under Gain/Loss (last column). Conceivably, you may buy to close this leg and roll it out to another strike or another expiry date. The closing action in this case would be to buy to close because it currently is an "open" position as part of a spread, as indicated by the -5 under Quantity. I only point this out to show you the versatility of options, and their tremendous potential to increase returns over time.

"LEAPS"

These are so-called Long-Term Equity Anticipation Securities, and are options contracts with expiration dates longer than 1 year. They function the same as shorter-term options, except they give the trader an opportunity to profit from longer-term changes in price. The premiums tend to be higher because they give the parent stock more time to achieve a desired price.

Strategy: "LEAPS" Call Options
OUTLOOK: Bullish (Stock Substitution)

If LEAPS provide an opportunity for longer-term positions, why would you wish to buy LEAPS Call options? Recall that call options allow the owner to buy a stock at a predetermined price by a predetermined date. By buying longer-term call options, you are effectively giving the parent stock more time to achieve your desired price. For example, if XYZ stock currently trades at $98, and you buy the LEAPS 100 strike, you are betting that XYZ will climb at least to $100 plus the premium you paid. From your prior exercises, recall that $100 is Out-of-The-Money; you are buying Time Value. You may wish to buy a call with only Time Value if your expectation is that the stock will make an appreciable enough climb well beyond the strike price to incorporate your premium. Recall from prior discussions that you are better off buying a call option with Intrinsic Value already built in – spend as little as possible on Time Value.

Strategy: "LEAP" Call Spreads
OUTLOOK: Bullish or Bearish

With a similar outlook as some of the shorter-term positions discussed above, the LEAPs Call Spreads can accomplish much the same result – either bullish or bearish – with less monitoring required. Because the premiums tend to be higher with longer-term options, it is often a useful strategy to "set it and forget it."

In the case of Bull Call Spreads, no margin is required as this is a debit spread. With Bear Call Spreads, the difference between the strike spread and the premium received will be held back as collateral.

In its Options Chains (located under the "Quotes" tab, OptionsXpress has many configurations of possible options positions, all described under "Type" with the dropdown arrow:

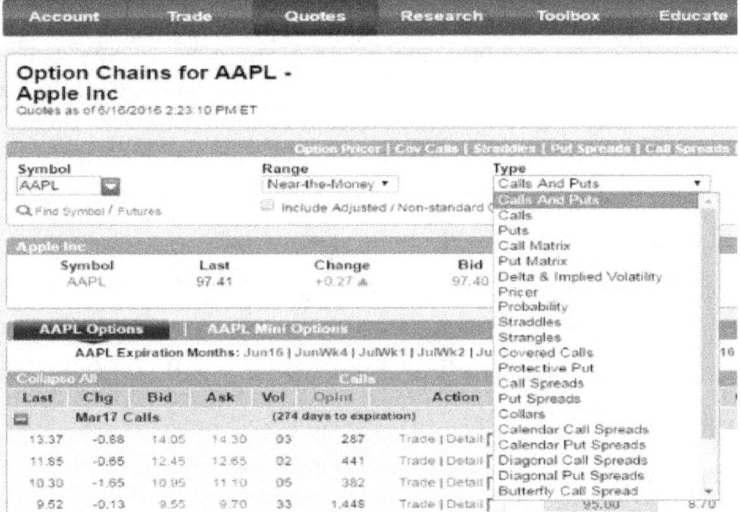

Select "Call Spreads" from the list. As you scroll down on the page, various expiration dates appear, with the first one above being Mar17 Calls, along with several possible spread trades. For example, the below prices represent the total spread prices for Call spreads, starting with 87.5/90, 90/92.5, 92.5/95, 95/97.5 and finally 97.5/100 (last row). If you are buying a 90/92.5 Call Spread you would pay (remember, it's a debit spread) 1.75 per share times the number of contracts. The options chains only show the price for a single share. Options contracts control 100 shares.

Bid	Ask	Break Even	Max Profit	Max Loss
				(274 days to expirat
1.40	1.90	89.40	$60.00	$190.00
1.30	1.75	91.75	$75.00	$175.00
1.20	1.60	94.10	$90.00	$160.00
1.10	1.45	96.45	$105.00	$145.00
1.00	1.30	98.80	$120.00	$130.00

Let's set up a debit Bull Call Spread for AAPL at 90/92.5 for 5 contracts:

BTO AAPL Mar17 90 Call x5
STO AAPL Mar17 92.5 Call x5
Total DEBIT (1.75 x5 x100) $875.00

In this case, since this is a debit spread, you will pay $875 (plus commission) to establish a Bull Call Spread expiring March 2017 with the strike prices of 90 and 92.5 for a 2.5 spread for which you will pay 1.75. Note that AAPL is currently trading at $98.94; therefore, if you recall from prior descriptions, the 90/92.5 call spread is In-The-Money.

What is the potential outcome? Assuming AAPL remains above the short (sold) leg (92.5) through expiration, you stand to make 2.5 from the 1.75 you paid. The potential profit, therefore, is 0.75 x5 x 100, or $375 (less commission). Your ROI (return on investment) is $375/$875=42.8%.

Notice that this sample Bull Call Spread was established by buying and selling In-The-Money strikes. If you must play with calls, that would be the safest choice because you are buying Intrinsic Value, rather than Time Value.

Test Your Knowledge

Price	Debit	Spread	Price	P/L
$95.23	1.6	90/92.5	$98.00	
$37.07	0.8	25/27.5	$30.27	
$43.00	1.3	45/50	$48.03	
$58.15	2.3	60/62.5	$60.70	

What would be your Profit or Loss depending on the above scenarios?

EPILOGUE

This is a short primer on Call Options. Study the principles herein and practice the exercises. The more comfortable you are with these concepts, the better mastery you will gain over your finances.

I invite you to study this book and the strategies presented, do the exercises, work them out on paper, and feel free to email me with your questions.

Website: Options For Newbies
http://selling-puts.blogspot.com
Email: OptionsForNewbies@outlook.com

LEXICON

AAPL – Stock symbol for Apple Computer.

Bearish – Having a negative outlook; expecting prices to decline.

Bid and ask

Bullish – Having a positive outlook; expecting prices to rise.

Calls – Call options; the right to buy stock at a predetermined price.

Collateral – Additional assets put up by a borrower against anticipated debt obligations. Used to reduce the risk to the broker.

Day trading – Usually involves trading in and out of securities and/or options several times in a day.

Delta – A measure of risk of an options price compared to its parent stock's price.

Derivatives – Any security whose price is dependent on its parent security.

Deep-In-The-Money – Any option whose premium is significantly above (for a call option) or significantly below (for a put option) than the current market price of its parent stock.

Earnings – How much profit a company produces during a specific period, usually reported as earnings per share (EP)

Exercise and Assignment – When an investor decides to call in a debt, he or she would exercise his option, while the seller of that option would have his option assigned.

Fundamentals – Any information that would be expected to affect the price of the stock, such as earnings, new products, new management, etc.

Intrinsic Value – The difference between the parent stock's price and the strike price.

Long – Buy, or any "owned" position.

Margin – Borrowed money used to buy securities or options.

Neutral – An outlook that is neither bullish nor bearish.

Option chains – A list of options prices for a given security.

Optionable – Any security that has exchange-traded options available. Not all publicly-traded companies have options on their stock.

Options – Financial derivatives sold by one entity and bought by another.

Position – Any trade.

Premium – The current price of an option.

Publicly-traded stocks – Any stocks traded on a public market for such securities.

Puts – Put options; the right to sell stock at a predetermined price.

Roll it up and out – The ability to exchange an options position to a different strike and/or different expiration date while it is still open.

Shares – Units of ownership in a company.

Short – Sell, or sold position.

Short-term trading – Any trade placed with a view to closing it in the short term, or having it expire in the short term.

Stock splits – A corporate action in which a company splits its outstanding shares into multiple units.

Stock symbols – An abbreviation of a company's name to list it for trading in a public market.

Stocks – Units of ownership in a corporation.

Strike price – The price at which an option can be exercised or assigned.

Technicals – A method used to analyze a security based on market action, such as price and chart studies.

The Greeks – A set of risk measures that indicate how exposed an option is to various components, such as time decay, volatility and the price of the parent stock.

Time to expiry – How much time is left before an option expires.

Time Value – The amount of the premium that is over the Intrinsic Value (Time Value=Prem. – Intrinsic Value)

Trading Levels – Levels of experience and amount of funding used by brokerage houses to assign risk.

Volatility – A technical indicator used to assess the anticipated range of price moves.

Wasting asset – Any asset that declines in value with the passage of time.

Writing – Selling.

ACRONYMS AND ABBREVIATIONS

The following lists the acronyms or expressions were used in this book. They are by no means comprehensive of all the jargon used in the industry. Indeed, jargon is often confounding, rather than clarifying; but the below acronyms are commonplace, and to the extent that I use them here, this list might prove useful.

ATM – At The Money

BCS – Bull Call Spread

bCS – Bear Call Spread

BPS – Bull Put Spread

bPS – Bear Put Spread

Cc – Covered Calls

DITM – deep-In-The-Money

ITM – In The Money

LEAPS – Long-Term Equity Anticipation Products

OTM – Out of The Money

*bCS and bPS are so noted to distinguish them from BCS and BPS. These acronyms are for the reader's edification. Some of these acronyms may not be universally recognized.

References

Allaire, Marc. *Understanding LEAPS*. New York: McGraw-Hill, 2003. Print.

"Characteristics & Risks of Standardized Options." *The Characteristics and Risks of Standardized Options (The Options Disclosure Document)*. N.p., n.d. Web. 17 Sept. 2015. <http://www.optionsclearing.com/about/publications/character-risks.jsp>.

Duarte, Joe. *Trading Options for Dummies*. N.p., 2015. Print.

Graham, Benjamin. *The Intelligent Investor*. New York: HarperBusiness Essentials, 2003. Print.

Hagstrom, Robert G. *The Warren Buffett Way*. New York, NY: Random House AudioBooks, 1995. Print.

Investopedia, https://en.wikipedia.org/wiki/Investopedia

Jensen, Greg. *Spread Trading*. Hoboken, N.J.: Wiley, 2009. Print.

Lefevre, Edwin. *Reminiscences of a Stock Operator*. New York: J. Wiley, 1994. Print.

McMillan, L. G. *McMillan on Options*. Hoboken, N.J.: John Wiley & Sons, 2004. Print.

"The Options Industry Council (OIC)." *The Options Industry Council (OIC)*. N.p., n.d. Web. 17 Sept. 2015. <http://www.optionseducation.org/>.

"OptionsXpress » Stocks, Options & Futures." *Options Trading, Stock Trading & Futures Trading at OptionsXpress*. N.p., n.d. Web. 17 Sept. 2015. <http://www.optionsxpress.com/>.

About The Author

I have been managing money, in one form or another, my entire life. While I was a single mother, money was extremely tight and I learned early how to conserve what I had and buy only the essentials. Later, I was introduced to the world of options trading, and fell in love with the process. I have been trading for the past 20 years, have written books on the subject, have been teaching a course on options trading, and have given public speeches on the same. In short, I am a passionate trader. Whatever expertise I may have did not come cheaply: I suffered devastating losses during the Dot Com era, an experience that has served me well as a form of an expensive post-graduate degree. Read my story below ("Memoirs of a Humbled Trader").

Throughout my life, I have learned to manage my finances through buying and selling real estate, for myself and as a Realtor for 10 years, negotiating prices, and dealing with various insurance brokers to settle claims. I have dealt with government programs as a landlord and have taught information technology at the college level.

Website: Options For Newbies
http://selling-puts.blogspot.com
Email: OptionsForNewbies@outlook.com

Memoirs of a Humbled Trader

The title of this book might be more appropriate as *Memoirs of a Humbled Trader*.

I began trading options in 1997. At the time, the stock market was ebullient with the Dot Coms, and it seemed that money was free for the taking. At first, I gingerly stepped into the water, but as my knowledge grew, so did my risk-taking, and happily, my returns. Eventually the market corrected, indeed, crashed. Most of the money I had made was in NASDAQ stocks on which I had sold naked puts (see Lexicon). This technique became my favorite, because it generated immediate cash into my account, while requiring a relatively minimal collateral. It worked well for a while. The technique itself was not at fault -- I was. There are certain safeguards that one must employ in any pursuit in life, not just financial, and it is only in retrospect, after suffering some serious bruising, that I recognize the error of my ways.

I remember September of 2000, when Intel (INTC) came out with some bad news and cratered. The market followed, but I was unconcerned, as were many of my fellow traders. We were riding high. We were happy. "Irrational exuberance" was the phrase Alan Greenspan had used in one of his speeches a couple of years earlier. Yep. We were exuberant. I'm not sure that any of us realized that we were irrational, too. How could we be irrational, when Yahoo! (YHOO) had a one-day price rally of $84!

One of the caveats of naked puts is to sell them only on stock we wish to own, because if it is "put" to you (assigned), you obligate yourself to buying it. I had a position of naked puts on YHOO expiring two years hence (the longer the time to expiration, the higher the premium) for a strike price of $150, this, when the stock was trading around $280. A strike price below the current market price is said to be out of the money for puts, and in the money for calls. In the case of YHOO sporting a market price of $280 and climbing monstrously each day, a strike of $150 two years later seemed very reasonable indeed. And so, I stayed in my position.

My troubles began the following year. By January of 2001, YHOO had begun to decline dramatically. In fact, it declined so far that it was "put" (assigned) to me. Being the irrationally exuberant person that I was, I decided to keep the stock at its substantially discounted price and write covered calls on it. How would I pay for it? By credit card, of course! Since I had a margin account, my out-of-pocket requirements were minimal, and those could "easily" be further mitigated by covered calls. The reasoning was intact; the technique was flawless. In retrospect, the decision to do so was not. But we all know about hindsight being 20/20, don't we? So I was now the proud owner of 1000 shares of a plummeting stock in a plummeting market, with a bulging credit card debt. Oy!

I decided to request an extension to file my taxes, which was granted to October of 2001. By that time, unfortunately, the stock market had declined much further than the previous September with the Intel calamity. Of course, so had my YHOO shares! But my credit card balance had not! A cardinal mistake I made in those days was not put aside a certain percentage of my winnings for taxes. And when the accountant presented me with my taxes owed, I was floored. We had suffered a stock market collapse; the Dot Com darlings were in the dog house; Greenspan was probably rubbing his hands in a self-satisfied gloat; and the heady thrill of daily price increases was a painful nightmare. Where was I going to find the money to pay the huge bill to the IRS? My credit card was maxed out - with YHOO, no less, a diminishing asset. I finally did pay the IRS by taking out a second mortgage on my house.

An ironic twist to this story is that, because of my financial woes at the time, I had very little cash on hand to pay my full IRS bill at one time. So, I set up an installment plan with the government. As luck would have it, my first check was insufficient! This, from someone financially savvy, fiscally responsible (notwithstanding my losses with options), and very nervous and compliant when it comes to matters of taxes. With that first insufficient funds payment, the IRS promptly issued a demand letter. And one does not mess with the IRS. After my initial shock at the insufficient funds (how was that possible? I set things up precisely with my bank!) I panicked. Enter the next savior: an equity loan on my house. I was granted the loan on top of my second mortgage, and promptly sped off a check to the IRS paying them in full. I was now the proud owner of a house mortgaged to the hilt, along with a credit card that was maxed out. Remember, too, that all that was occurring very soon after the 9/11 attacks, and the economy was shaky, with new rules and dwindling tourists; and tourism was my husband's occupation.

Fast forward to today...

Naked puts remain my favorite strategy. I now have my experience to buttress my ego. I'm also much closer to retirement, and therefore less able to swing for the fences with abandon (though that sure was fun!). I now put safeguards in place -- and lest you should be rubbing your own hands in smug satisfaction, this blog fills such a purpose precisely: to identify those very safeguards for myself, as well as my readership.

Options are a financial tool, just as are certificates of deposit and Treasurys. And as a tool, they can enhance your life immeasurably, but they require an understanding of all their permutations. It is my wish to impart to the reader whatever lessons I have learned the hard way, and demystify their power.

www.ingramcontent.com/pod-product-compliance
Lightning Source LLC
Chambersburg PA
CBHW071611170526
45166CB00003B/1060